Drawing Conclusions

Middle

The Jamestown Comprehension Skills Series with Writing Activities

THIRD EDITION

JAMESTOWN PUBLISHERS

a division of NTC/CONTEMPORARY PUBLISHING GROUP
Lincolnwood, Illinois USA

ISBN: 0-8092-0248-4

Published by Jamestown Publishers,
a division of NTC/Contemporary Publishing Group, Inc.
©2000 NTC/Contemporary Publishing Group, Inc.,
4255 West Touhy Avenue, Lincolnwood Illinois 60712-1975 U.S.A.

6 7 8 9 10 11 12 117 09 08 07 06

INTRODUCTION

The Comprehension Skills Series has been prepared to help students develop specific reading comprehension skills. Each book is completely self-contained. There is no separate answer key or instruction manual. Throughout the book, clear and concise directions guide the student through the lessons and exercises.

The titles of the Comprehension Skills books match the labels found on comprehension questions in other Jamestown textbooks. The student who is having difficulty with a particular kind of question can use the matching Comprehension Skills book for extra instruction and practice to correct the specific weakness.

Each book in the Comprehension Skills Series is divided into five parts.

1. **Explanation:** Part One (p. 5) clearly defines, explains, and illustrates the specific skill. It begins with a Preview Quiz to get students thinking about the material that will be presented.

2. **Instruction:** Part Two (p. 8) offers an interesting and informative lesson presented in clear, readable language. This section also utilizes the preview technique introduced in Part One, which requires students to anticipate and respond to the subject matter.

3. **Sample Exercise:** Part Three (p. 18) consists of a sample exercise with questions. The sample exercise is designed to prepare students for the work required in the following section. Students should read and follow the instructions carefully. When they have finished the exercise, they should read the analysis following it. For each question, there is a step-by-step explanation of why one answer is correct, and why the others are not. Students are urged to consult the teacher if they need extra help before proceeding to Part Four.

4. Practice Exercises: Part Four (p. 23) contains twenty practice exercises with questions. Squares (■) bordering the exercises indicate the level of difficulty. The greater the number of squares, the greater the difficulty of the passage. Students are advised to read the instructions and complete the practice exercises thoughtfully and carefully.

5. Writing Activities: Part Five (p. 49) contains writing activities that help students apply the skills they have learned in earlier parts of the book. Students should read and follow the instructions carefully. Many activities encourage students to work together cooperatively. The teacher may want to discuss these activities in class.

Each book also contains an Answer Key, which can be found after the Writing Activities. Students can record their scores and monitor their progress on the chart following the Answer Key.

Understanding Conclusions

Preview Quiz 1

As a preview of what will be discussed in Part One, try to complete this sentence:

A conclusion is a decision about

    a. what decisions can be made based on the stated facts.

    b. what may have led to the stated facts.

    c. how believable an argument is.

Begin reading Part One to discover how conclusions are different from other decisions.

Writers often mean more than they say. They do not directly state everything they want you to understand. They leave something unsaid, even though they think it is important. Sometimes, for instance, conclusions are left unstated.

What is a conclusion? A conclusion is a decision or opinion you make that is based on the facts you have read.

Why do writers leave you to draw your own conclusions? They may have several reasons.

- It may not occur to them that the conclusion has to be stated. They may think that everyone—including you—will know it.

- They may want *you* to draw the conclusion. After leading you in the direction of a conclusion, a writer may stop and leave you on your own. The writer feels that if *you* draw the conclusion, you will be convinced that it is right.

- The writer's purpose for writing may be different from your purpose for reading. In this case, the writer does not state some conclusions because they do not suit his or her purpose. There is no reason for the writer to state the conclusions.

As you can see, there are many reasons why you may have to draw your own conclusions. This is why you need to know how to draw conclusions when reading. Only then can you be sure of fully understanding what you read.

Let's see what a reasonable and sound conclusion is. First read this paragraph.

> Severe storm warnings have been posted along the Gulf Coast. Hurricane Gillian is expected to strike land near Galveston. Forecasters expect the storm to strike before midnight. Electricity outages are likely. Water supplies may be contaminated by seawater. Extremely high tides are expected.

A good reader can draw several conclusions from the paragraph. The reader should ask, "What is implied by the stated facts?"

- *Severe storm warnings have been posted.*
  This implies that boats should stay in port.

- *The storm is expected to strike near Galveston.*
  This implies that people there should prepare for it.

- *The storm will strike before midnight.*
  This implies that people should be ready before then.

- *Electricity outages are likely.*
  This implies that people should have candles and flashlights ready.

- *Water supplies may be contaminated.*
  This implies that people should store fresh water now.

Each of these is a reasonable conclusion drawn from the paragraph.

Drawing a Conclusion

How can you draw a conclusion? First, recognize cause-and-effect relationships. Much of our thinking is based on cause and effect. We know from experience that certain events cause others—one thing makes another thing happen.

You take a bite of hot pizza. The pizza burns your mouth. The hot pizza is the cause. The burn is the effect. The burn makes you feel pain. This time, the burn is the cause. Pain is the effect. Biting into hot pizza causes a burned mouth. A burned mouth causes pain. Remember that a good reader asks, "What do the stated facts imply?" What does biting into a hot pizza imply? A burned mouth. What does a burned mouth imply? Pain.

There are other ways to state these cause-and-effect relationships. A writer may express them in any of the following ways.

- Eating hot pizza implies a burned mouth.
- Because the pizza is hot, you will burn your mouth.
- The pizza is hot. Therefore, you will burn your mouth.
- If the pizza is hot, then you will burn your mouth.

Often, however, writers leave out the effects. They state the cause, but leave it to you to decide what the effect will be. You do this, too. You might say to a friend, "Watch out. This pizza is hot!" You state the cause: hot pizza. You don't state the effect: a burned mouth. Your friend has to draw a conclusion by asking, "What does the stated fact imply?"

Your first step in drawing a conclusion is to be aware of cause-and-effect relationships. Look for causes that imply certain effects. Try it with this passage.

Most of us have had cramps of one kind or another. A cramp is a contraction of muscles. Some cramps are brought on by muscle strain in cold weather. Other cramps come from overwork in great heat. Firefighters may get cramps of that type. Their bodies become overheated, and they perspire heavily. That makes them lose salt and water. Treatment varies according to the type of cramp. One patient may need cool air, salt tablets, and water. Another may need a heating pad on the cramp.

Notice some causes that imply certain effects:

Some cramps are brought on by muscle strain in cold weather.
Other cramps come from overwork in great heat.

Those are causes. The writer has left their effects unstated. The last part of the paragraph includes the effects.

Some cramps are brought on by muscle strain in cold weather.

What does this imply?

The patient may need a heating pad on the cramp.

Other cramps come from overwork in great heat.

What does this imply?

These patients may need cool air, salt tablets, and water.

Preview Quiz 3

As a preview of what will be discussed next, try to answer this question:

Why should you consider all the possible conclusions in what you read?

    a. Each fact can lead to only one conclusion.

    b. One set of facts may lead to several conclusions.

    c. Most facts have no conclusion at all.

Continue reading to discover the correct answer.

You should consider all possible conclusions before settling on one. Why? One cause may have many effects. Therefore, one set of facts may lead to several conclusions.

This brings up an important point about reading. Good readers always think while they read. They consider the ideas, weigh them, and try to decide where they lead. They think about what the passage suggests and what it implies. Good readers keep an open mind. They do not jump to conclusions. Instead, they stretch their thinking and consider all the possibilities. Only then do they settle on the most likely conclusions.

The next passage will show how important it is to consider all the conclusions. It mentions some qualities of ducks. As you read, watch for causes. Think about the effects they imply.

Most ducks have light, hollow bones. Light bones make it easier for ducks that feed on the surface of the water to stay afloat. Diving ducks, however, often chase fish under water. Diving ducks have much heavier bones than surface-feeding ducks.

Many statements in the paragraph are causes that imply certain effects. Read the next two sentences.

Most ducks have light, hollow bones.
Diving ducks have heavy bones.

What effects do these causes imply? Try to think of as many as you can. Review the paragraph. Brainstorm. Jot down a list of likely effects. Save your list.

Now look for causes in this paragraph.

Most drakes (male ducks) are brightly colored. However, at the end of the mating season most drakes molt. That is, they lose their old feathers. Without their flight feathers, the drakes are unable to fly. They also lose their bright coloring and turn a drab brown.

Did you spot these causes?

Most drakes are brightly colored.
Drakes can't fly when they lose their old feathers.
The drakes turn a drab brown when they molt.

What effects do *these* causes imply? Again, try to think of as many as you can. Jot down a list of them. Save the list. You will evaluate your lists of effects in the next section.

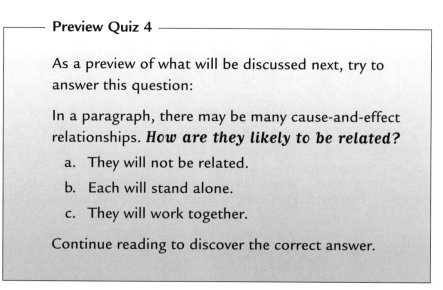

Preview Quiz 4

As a preview of what will be discussed next, try to answer this question:

In a paragraph, there may be many cause-and-effect relationships. *How are they likely to be related?*
   a. They will not be related.
   b. Each will stand alone.
   c. They will work together.

Continue reading to discover the correct answer.

The thoughts in a paragraph work together. They develop a topic, theme, or idea. For this reason, you will usually find that causes and effects work together, too. When you see how the causes and effects work together, you may see that they lead to an overall conclusion. At the end of the last section, you listed possible effects of causes in two paragraphs about ducks. Let's begin with the first paragraph. Your list of effects may have included these:

Cause: Most ducks have light, hollow bones.
Effects: They float very well.
         They can swim quickly.
         They can feed on the surface of the water.

Cause: Diving ducks have heavy bones.
Effects: They can swim under water.
         They can chase fish under water.

Think about these effects. You should begin to see a pattern. Most ducks are surface-feeders. Diving ducks can feed under water. What can you conclude from these facts?

Conclusions: Ducks with light bones can only feed on the surface.
Diving ducks can feed on the surface or catch fish under water.

The causes and effects work together. Now let's look at the second paragraph. Your list of effects may have included these:

Cause: Most drakes are brightly colored.
Effects: They are attractive. They are easy to see.

Cause: Drakes are unable to fly when they molt.
Effects: They cannot travel far.
They cannot escape easily from enemies.

Cause: The drakes lose their bright coloring and turn a drab brown.
Effects: They are not as attractive.
They blend in with other ducks.

Again, you should see a pattern. Brightly colored ducks are easy to see. Without their flight feathers drakes can't easily escape from their enemies. Drakes with drab coloring blend in with other brown ducks. What do these facts imply?

Conclusion: Drakes can easily hide from their enemies when they molt.

From your work with these paragraphs, you should see that it is important to consider all the likely conclusions. Keep an open mind. Consider all the possibilities. Then draw a conclusion.

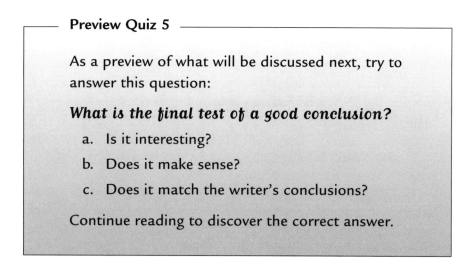

Sometimes you will have to draw a conclusion from an unstated main idea. The writing will not make a direct statement that leads to the conclusion. How can you tell if such a conclusion is a good one? Test it by deciding whether it makes sense. Making sense is the final test of a good conclusion. Try it with this paragraph:

Most earthquakes occur when rock slides along a crack, or "fault," in the earth's crust. The sliding causes vibrations. The vibrations move through the ground like waves through water. These "seismic waves" cause some areas to rise and others to fall. Cities are most affected when the waves make buildings collapse. Flexible buildings can move with these waves. They bend with them, like trees bending in the wind. Rigid buildings do not bend. They are like stiff, dead branches. Buildings on solid rock tend to move with the rock. They "ride the waves" as if on a surfboard, and the rock absorbs some of the shock. Buildings in loose earth shake more violently.

The main idea is not stated. It is this:

> Seismic waves created by an earthquake cause
> damage to buildings.

Within the passage are several facts that lead to conclusions. Here are some, along with some conclusions they imply:

        Fact: Most earthquakes occur when rock slides
                       along a "fault."
Conclusion: The greatest danger is near a fault.

        Fact: The vibrations move through the ground
                       like waves through water.
Conclusion: Damage may occur far away.

        Fact: Flexible buildings can bend with these
                       waves, like trees bending in the wind.
Conclusions: Flexible buildings are less likely to collapse.

        Fact: Rigid buildings are like stiff, dead branches.
Conclusion: Rigid buildings are more likely to collapse.

        Fact: Buildings on solid rock move with the rock,
                       which absorbs some of the shock.
Conclusion: Buildings on rock aren't as likely to be
                       damaged.

        Fact: Buildings in loose earth shake more
                       violently.
Conclusion: Buildings in loose earth are more likely to
                       be damaged.

From the main idea and the details, you can draw an overall conclusion.

> Flexible buildings on solid rock are safest in earthquakes.

As you read, follow these steps to draw conclusions.

- Watch for causes. Ask yourself what effects or conclusions they imply.
- Stretch your thinking. Go beyond the obvious. Try to imagine what all the possible conclusions are.
- Remember that one cause may have many effects. Therefore, one set of facts may lead to several conclusions.
- Don't draw a final conclusion until you have explored all of the possible conclusions. Put your findings together. Decide which outcomes seem most likely.
- Finally, draw your conclusions. Decide whether they make sense. Remember that making sense is the final test of a conclusion.

PART THREE

Sample Exercise

The exercise on the next page is a sample exercise. Its purpose is to show how the information you have studied in Parts One and Two can be put to use in reading.

A second purpose of the sample exercise is to preview the twenty exercises that appear in Part Four. Reading the sample passage and answering the sample questions will help you get off to a good start.

The answers to all the questions are fully explained. Reasons are given showing why the correct answers are the best answers and where the wrong answers are faulty. In addition, the text describes the thinking you might do as you work through the exercise correctly.

Complete the sample exercise carefully and thoughtfully. Do not go on to Part Four until you are certain that you understand what a conclusion is and how to draw accurate conclusions.

┌─── Sample Exercise ──────────────────────────────────

On April 15, 1912, the *Titanic,* the largest ship in the world, struck an iceberg and sank. More than 1,500 people died in the early morning darkness off Newfoundland. The luxury liner was making its first trip from England to New York City when the tragedy occurred. Only 705 people were saved from the supposedly unsinkable ship. Earlier in the night, the captain of the ship had been warned that icebergs had been seen in the area. But the big liner sped on through the darkness. It headed swiftly toward its grave. At 11:40 p.m. the giant ship rammed the white, silent giant of nature. A gash 300 feet (more than 91 meters) long opened the side of the ship to the sea. In less than three hours the ship was swallowed up by the dark and silent North Atlantic.

1. Why did the *Titanic* speed on through the darkness after iceberg warnings were received?
   a. The *Titanic* was poorly made.
   b. The captain paid no attention to the warning.
   c. The iceberg moved very quickly.
   d. The captain had military training.

2. From the fact that the North Atlantic was "dark and silent," you can conclude that
   a. icebergs are rarely seen in the North Atlantic.
   b. several ships rushed to the aid of the *Titanic.*
   c. stormy weather played no part in the disaster.
   d. many children died in the disaster.

3. From the main idea, you can conclude that
   a. the *Titanic* carried too many people.
   b. the people who thought the *Titanic* was unsinkable hadn't taken human error into account.
   c. passenger traffic by ship in the North Atlantic was abandoned following the *Titanic* disaster.
   d. sabotage was a likely cause of the sinking.

4. Underline the sentences that support the conclusion that the *Titanic* must have carried more than 2,200 people.

Answers and Explanations

1. To answer this question, you must recognize a cause-and-effect relationship. You are given the effect. You must choose the cause. Read each possible cause and decide which implies the ship's speeding on.

The best answer is *b*. The captain paid no attention to the warning. You can check this for yourself. Think of a sentence that states the cause-and-effect relationship: *Because* the captain paid no attention to the warning, the *Titanic* sped on.

Answer *a* is wrong because poor construction would not cause a ship to speed on after a warning.

Answer *c* is wrong because a quickly moving iceberg would not cause the ship to speed on either.

Answer *d* is wrong because there is no reason why military training would make the captain order the ship to speed on.

2. Completing this sentence requires you to find a conclusion implied by a cause. The cause is the fact that the sea was dark and silent. In your mind, construct a sentence in which the cause begins with *if.* Then look for the best ending to it. If the North Atlantic were dark and silent, then . . .

The best answer is *c*. Stormy weather played no part in the disaster. Try this at the end of the "if . . . then . . ." sentence.

Answer *a* is wrong because darkness and silence do not have anything to do with icebergs.

Answer *b* is wrong because ships bring light and sound.

Answer *d* is wrong because darkness and silence do not suggest children.

3. To complete this sentence, first decide what the main idea of the paragraph is. The passage seems to lead to the idea that the *Titanic* sank because the captain ignored warnings.

The best answer is *b*. It was the captain's error that led to the disaster.

Answer *a* is wrong because we are not told that the ship was overloaded.

Answer *c* is wrong because the paragraph includes nothing on this topic.

Answer *d* is wrong because there is no mention of sabotage.

4. Here you are told to find sentences that support a certain conclusion. You are told to find the cause of a certain effect. To do so, review the paragraph to find a likely cause. Then test it by adding the word *because* and seeing whether it implies the effect. The best answers are these sentences:

More than 1,500 people died in the early morning darkness off Newfoundland. Only 705 people were saved from the supposedly unsinkable ship.

Try the test:

Because more than 1,500 people died and 705 people were saved, the *Titanic* must have carried more than 2,200 people.

If you had trouble answering these questions, look over the sample exercise and questions again. If, after that, you still do not understand the answers and the reasons for them, check with your teacher before going on.

PART FOUR

Practice Exercises

- The twenty practice exercises that follow will help you put to use your ability to draw conclusions.

- Each exercise is just like the sample exercise you completed in Part Three.

- Read each passage well. Answer carefully and thoughtfully the four questions with it.

- Correct your answers using the Answer Key at the back of the book. Mark your scores on the chart on page 64 before going on to the next exercise.

— Practice Exercise *1* —————————————

Abraham Lincoln had a tadpole. It wasn't the kind that has a slender tail and lives in ponds. Lincoln's tadpole lived in the White House. His "tadpole" was his young son, Thomas. One day when Thomas was a baby, Lincoln looked at him and chuckled. "He looks like a tadpole," Lincoln said. From that day on, the baby was called Tad—short for tadpole. He was known by that name to the nation.

Also known to the nation were Tad's pranks. He thought up so many tricks to play on people that he kept the White House in confusion.

One afternoon while Mrs. Lincoln was entertaining guests in the East Room, Tad rushed in with his two pet goats. They were tied to a chair. Tad was holding the reins and sitting in the chair. The ladies gasped. Before they really knew what was happening, Tad and the goats ran out of the room.

1. From Tad's behavior, you can conclude that
   a. Lincoln treated his son cruelly.
   b. Lincoln liked to be with children.
   c. Tad hated his nickname.
   d. Tad often got himself into trouble.

2. From Lincoln's attitude toward his son, you can conclude that Lincoln
   a. did not get along well with his children.
   b. was troubled by affairs of state.
   c. had a sense of humor.
   d. believed in strong discipline.

3. From the last paragraph you can conclude that
   a. Lincoln made any situation a learning experience.
   b. animals were mistreated in Lincoln's day.
   c. Tad often did the unexpected.
   d. Mrs. Lincoln held many parties in the East Room.

4. Underline two sentences that imply that the public was interested in the president's family.

Practice Exercise **2**

The koala bear of Australia is a living teddy bear. Its thick coat of gray fur is just as soft as the beloved toy. The koala has a large head, big ears, and small, dark eyes that look at you without expression. Its nose, as black as patent leather, seems too big for the rest of its face.

The koala is a gentle little animal. It is almost defenseless. Only its color protects it from enemies.

The koala makes no nest. It just sits in the forked branches of a tree. Unlike a bird, it cannot balance itself with its tail—because it has no tail. It likes eucalyptus (yoo-kuh-LIHP-tuhs) trees best because it lives entirely on the leaves of the tree. Sometimes the supply of its special diet is used up. Rather than seek food elsewhere, the koala will stay in its own area and starve to death.

1. From the main idea of the first paragraph, you can conclude that people find the koala bear

a. cute.   c. hideous.

b. frightening.   d. annoying.

2. From the main idea of the second paragraph, you can conclude that the koala bear

a. attacks other animals viciously.

b. is more likely to run than fight.

c. is most afraid of snakes.

d. is the rarest animal in Australia.

3. From the main idea of the third paragraph, you can conclude that you are most likely to find koalas

a. throughout Asia.

b. curled up in their nests hibernating.

c. in the vast deserts of the Australian outback.

d. only where there are eucalyptus trees.

4. Underline the sentence that supports the conclusion that the koala is not dangerous to tourists.

Practice Exercise 3

In many places today, clams are not safe to eat because they come from dirty waters. However, during the first year of the Plymouth Colony, clams saved the Pilgrims.

Upon arriving, the Pilgrims dug big holes into the sides of hills to make "dugouts." They put up sod walls and roofs of tree bark. Each dugout would keep a family safe through the winter until the Pilgrims could build log cabins in the spring.

How would they feed themselves until then? The Pilgrims had muskets and crossbows, but not many of the people were good shots. They had fishing lines, but the hooks were too big for the fish in shallow Plymouth Bay. Only half of the 102 Pilgrims lived through that first winter. They all might have died if it had not been for the clam. The clam was a lifesaver in the truest sense of the word.

1. From the fact that most of the Pilgrims were not good shots, you can conclude that
   a. crossbows are difficult to aim.
   b. religious convictions kept them from learning.
   c. the Pilgrims came well prepared.
   d. they would not be good at hunting game.

2. From the fact that the Pilgrims brought large fishing hooks with them, you can conclude that they
   a. wanted to put the hooks to many uses.
   b. could not buy small hooks in England.
   c. had to take whatever was given to them.
   d. expected to fish in deep ocean waters.

3. From the passage as a whole and the fact that clams saved the Pilgrims, you can conclude that
   a. clams are still popular in New England.
   b. digging clams is easier than hunting game.
   c. clams were not safe to eat in the Pilgrims' time.
   d. the Pilgrims' dugouts were nearly useless.

4. Underline a sentence that implies that the dugouts were only temporary shelters.

Practice Exercise 4

At one time or another, most people suffer from hiccups. Few people realize that hiccups can be caused by different things. A hiccup, for example, can be caused by a full stomach or by tumors in the stomach. Or it can be brought on by drinking something hot or cold too quickly.

A hiccup is really the reverse of coughing. The diaphragm contracts and pulls air across the vocal cords. From there the air rushes suddenly into the lungs. This makes the "hic-uhp" sound.

Sometimes hiccups are so violent or long lasting that medical help is necessary. In most cases, however, they stop quickly with no side effects.

1. From the fact that tumors in the stomach can cause hiccups, you can conclude that
   a. a person with frequent hiccups should see a doctor.
   b. hiccups are always harmless.
   c. standing on your head is sure to cure hiccups.
   d. doctors do not take hiccups seriously.

2. From the first paragraph, you can conclude that hiccups occur most often
   a. during moments of crisis.
   b. during meals.
   c. in times of excitement.
   d. in times of sadness.

3. From the passage as a whole, you can conclude that hiccups signal
   a. overworked lungs.
   b. a weak diaphragm.
   c. strained vocal cords.
   d. an irritated stomach.

4. Underline a sentence that supports the conclusion that hiccups are not usually a serious illness.

Practice Exercise 5

One amazing "water miser" of the desert is the spadefoot toad. Most people do not think of a toad as a desert dweller at all because they know that toads must be born in water. The mystery is solved if one knows something about deserts. After a hard spring rain, a few puddles form here and there. The female spadefoot toad looks for these puddles, and there she lays her eggs. If the puddles dry up by the next day, the eggs don't hatch. But if the puddles last even two days, they are suddenly full of tiny tadpoles. And if a little water remains for just two weeks, these desert tadpoles are ready to live in the hottest parts of the desert. From then on the toad's only moisture comes from the insects it eats.

1. The passage as a whole implies that
   a. people are not interested in toads.
   b. people know more about frogs than toads.
   c. spadefoot toads need water but don't drink it.
   d. spadefoot toads leave the desert in the fall.

2. From the passage as a whole, you can conclude that the spadefoot toad is called a "water miser" because it
   a. needs no water at all to survive.
   b. stores water in its home.
   c. steals water from other animals.
   d. needs very little water to survive.

3. From the explanation of conditions for hatching, you can conclude that toad eggs
   a. hatch as soon as water touches them.
   b. cannot survive dry periods.
   c. need at least two days in water to hatch.
   d. are usually eaten by insects before they hatch.

4. Underline a sentence that gives an example of a mistaken conclusion.

Practice Exercise 6

Somewhere out in the ocean a blue whale is swimming. It is a great mass of moving blubber. It is the mightiest animal that has ever lived. Its mouth is so big that it can hold a small table and chairs. Yet this giant beast with the giant mouth hasn't any teeth. Instead, it has hundreds of thin plates in its mouth. Its throat is so small that nothing larger than an orange can get through it.

It is lucky for such a toothless creature that there is plankton in the water. Plankton is the rich, thick "soup" of the sea, and it is the blue whale's food. It floats near the surface of the water and drifts with the currents. Plankton is made up of the tiniest plants and animals in the sea. The blue whale swims with its mouth open. That way the whale can filter out plankton from the water.

1. Which one of the following conclusions is supported by the passage?
   a. Plankton is a nourishing food.
   b. The blue whale is a feeble creature.
   c. Blue whales eat lobsters.
   d. The blue whale is a threat to people.

2. The passage supports the conclusion that
   a. the blue whale prefers to eat shrimp more than crabs.
   b. most fish have no reason to fear the blue whale.
   c. the blue whale is the only toothless whale.
   d. lobsters and crabs live in masses of plankton.

3. From the size of the whale's throat, you can conclude that the whale
   a. cannot swallow large fish.
   b. can eat just about anything.
   c. probably breathes through its throat.
   d. tires easily.

4. Underline the sentence that supports the conclusion that the blue whale eats both animals and plants.

Practice Exercise 7

People who like to dive for buried treasure and sunken ships often meet in Key West, Florida. From there, in pairs or in groups, they scatter to their favorite diving spots. The powdery sands of the Florida Keys are surrounded by clear waters. These waters are filled with marine life of many kinds and colors. Yet the clear water can be dangerous. It is often deeper than it looks. Sometimes there is coral with razor-sharp edges.

Often divers find the old ships they are after. However, boats on the bottom of the ocean are not complete ships with colorful fish swimming through them. Shipworms have eaten away the wood, and any metal is coated with coral. Sand covers many parts of the ship. The trained diver sifts through the debris to uncover gold and silver coins.

1. You can conclude that
   a. the waters off Florida are probably not badly polluted.
   b. shipworms attack divers.
   c. sharks bother divers.
   d. the beaches of Key West are covered with shells.

2. You can conclude that most sunken ships are
   a. found intact.
   b. fully preserved by the salt water.
   c. found in one area.
   d. hidden from the diver's view.

3. Which statement best supports the conclusion that Key West is a favorite meeting spot for treasure hunters?
   a. Key West hotels are modern and comfortable.
   b. There are many varieties of fish in the waters.
   c. Many ships are known to have sunk in the area.
   d. Coral is easy to find in and around Key West.

4. Underline a sentence that supports the conclusion that swimming near coral may be dangerous.

— Practice Exercise *8* —————————————————

Have you ever heard of farms for wild animals? The University of Alaska has one. It's an experimental farm that raises musk oxen. At one time, the oxen were dying out, and few of the animals were left. Now because of the work going on at the farm, the musk oxen have not only been saved but also been put to work.

Finding musk oxen was a tough job. The animals were few and far between. They are easily frightened. Their only natural enemy is the wolf. When wolves come close, the oxen defend themselves by forming a ring with their sharp horns pointed outward. This makes the job of capturing them all the harder. The few musk oxen that could be captured were taken to the farm to begin breeding under carefully arranged conditions.

It is natural that the musk ox should be the animal farmed in Alaska. It is used to cold weather, and its wool makes excellent cloth.

1. The passage leads the reader to conclude that
   a. wild animal farms are unusual.
   b. the musk ox is found all over the world.
   c. wolves are afraid of musk oxen.
   d. the flesh of the musk ox tastes like beef.

2. The musk ox is
   a. easy to breed.
   b. a threat to the existence of the wolf.
   c. easy to train.
   d. difficult to capture.

3. From the evidence in the passage, you can conclude that the University of Alaska's experimental farm
   a. has been successful.
   b. has now been closed.
   c. will begin raising other animals as well.
   d. has caused a drop in the wolf population.

4. Underline a sentence that allows the reader to conclude that musk oxen can work together as a group.

Practice Exercise *9*

The powerful Siberian husky is an Arctic sled dog. Many Eskimos still use huskies to get from one place to another. Even though the snowmobile and the airplane have taken the husky's place in the larger villages, Eskimos in most places still need their dogs. They think of their dogs as their transportation and their friends. The huskies can drag their master and a heavy load much farther than even a snowmobile can.

In the far north, planes sometimes cannot fly because of the cold. But a team of healthy huskies is hardly ever stopped by the cold. This is the way it has been for centuries. Huskies were known to explorers in the fifteenth century, and Eskimos must have made use of them centuries before that.

1. The selection allows the reader to conclude that the husky dog is valuable for its
   a. hunting skills.
   b. strength.
   c. friendship.
   d. loyalty.

2. In larger Eskimo villages the husky is
   a. receiving a new type of training.
   b. bred for sale in the United States.
   c. cared for by children.
   d. being replaced.

3. From the example in the passage, we can conclude that
   a. people can control what happens to them.
   b. the old ways are sometimes the best ways.
   c. new ideas save work.
   d. people are easily satisfied.

4. Underline a sentence that allows the reader to conclude that Eskimos must take excellent care of their dogs.

Practice Exercise *10*

Long, long ago there were no yardsticks, rulers, or metersticks. When people first began to measure things, they used their own fingers or their own hands. They may have even used their arms or feet. "This is a three-finger spearhead," a person might have said, or "This fish is as long as my foot put down two times." When people measured things, they were using fingers and feet just as we use inch and foot markings on a yardstick. Today, whether we are measuring things by inches or by meters, we are using standard units of measurement. Imagine early people using their feet as a foot measurement; you can see the problems they would have had. One person might have been tall and had long feet. Another might have been short and had short feet. That is why standard units of measurement are used.

1. People probably first measured things with their hands rather than with sticks because
   a. hands were more accurate.
   b. the hand was a standard unit of measurement.
   c. using their hands was natural.
   d. sticks were hard to find.

2. If people with different-sized feet measured the same thing in "feet," then
   a. the true length would be the average.
   b. they would get the same results.
   c. we would know the real length of a foot.
   d. they would disagree about the size.

3. Because measurements are made with standard units,
   a. the foot has been replaced by the meter.
   b. measurements agree no matter who makes them.
   c. all spearheads are made the same size.
   d. the word *inch* has been made from the old word for *hand*.

4. Underline the sentences that imply the reason for not using parts of the body for measuring.

Practice Exercise *11*

The next time you have to take medicine but don't like the taste, try this: first chill the inside of your mouth by placing an ice cube in it. You won't taste the medicine at all.

Very hot and very cold foods can change your sense of taste. Heat, of course, increases your ability to taste. You can taste very small amounts of sugar in hot coffee. But a lot more sugar is needed to make ice cream and other cold foods taste sweet.

Your sense of smell is another thing that can change your sense of taste. You can prove this by drinking chocolate while holding your nose. You'll find that it doesn't taste much like chocolate. If you really want a surprise, hold your nose and close your eyes while somebody gives you a bite of onion and a bite of apple. You won't be able to taste the difference.

1. According to this selection, a person trying to lose weight may find that the most damaging foods are
   a. cold desserts.
   b. hot drinks.
   c. breads.
   d. warm puddings.

2. When the sense of smell is blocked,
   a. foods taste sour.
   b. foods taste somewhat hotter.
   c. foods taste very sweet.
   d. different foods may taste the same.

3. The reader can conclude that
   a. the sense of sight is most important in the enjoyment of food.
   b. most people do not like foods that are too hot.
   c. several senses are used to enjoy food.
   d. onions have the strongest flavor of any food.

4. Underline the sentence that supports the conclusion drawn in number 1.

— Practice Exercise *12* —

There are only two places in the world today where there is as much ice as there was during ice ages of the past. One is Greenland. The other is Antarctica, the large body of land at the south polar region.

Except for a narrow strip around its shores, Greenland lies buried under a sheet of permanent ice. The ice is thousands of feet thick, so that only the tops of the highest mountains extend above it. From this ice cap huge glaciers pour into the sea. Icebergs break from these glaciers and drift into the open seas. Sometimes they move thousands of miles to the south before they melt.

The famous liner *Titanic* struck such an iceberg. The shipbuilders were sure that the *Titanic* could not sink because of its special design. But the damage was so great that the huge ship sank to the bottom of the ocean.

1. Why do fewer glaciers exist today than during the ice ages?
   a. Less snow falls in Antarctica now.
   b. Glaciers now move into the open seas.
   c. Earth has warmed up.
   d. Icebreakers keep polar areas clear of ice.

2. You can conclude that most towns in Greenland have been built
   a. in central regions.
   b. on the slopes of northern mountains.
   c. on open plains.
   d. in coastal areas.

3. From the air, Antarctica probably looks like
   a. tiny peaked islands in a sea of ice.
   b. a vast mass of ice and snow.
   c. mountains dotted with tiny farms.
   d. a rocky, barren continent.

4. Underline the sentence that tells why designers concluded that the *Titanic* was unsinkable.

— Practice Exercise **13** —

John Wilkes Booth belonged to a famous family of actors. His father, Junius Brutus Booth, was a successful English actor who moved to the United States in 1821. John's brother, Edwin Thomas Booth, is remembered as one of the greatest actors in the history of American theater.

John Wilkes Booth was also a promising actor. But today he is remembered as the man who murdered Abraham Lincoln. Booth sympathized with the South during the Civil War. He and his friends plotted to kill Lincoln and several other government officials. On April 14, 1865, he shot the president during a performance at Ford's Theatre in Washington, D.C. Although he broke his leg when he leaped from the president's box, Booth managed to escape on horseback. Twelve days later federal troops trapped him in a barn in Port Royal, Virginia, where Booth was shot to death.

1. Before he murdered the president, John Wilkes Booth was
   a. less famous than his brother.
   b. more famous than his brother.
   c. his father's favorite son.
   d. completely unknown.

2. From the statements in the passage, you can conclude that Booth
   a. fought in the war.
   b. needed money.
   c. was a poor actor.
   d. hated Lincoln.

3. You can assume that Lincoln
   a. admired Booth's acting skills.
   b. sympathized with the South during the war.
   c. had not been warned of a possible attack.
   d. died instantly.

4. Underline two sentences that support the answer to number 1.

Practice Exercise 14

The waterworks of ancient Rome were so advanced that they make even some of today's systems seem crude by comparison. An early Roman architect, Vitruvius (vuh-TROO-vee-uhs), was concerned about water quality. He demanded that his drinking water be boiled and kept in silver tanks. The water was even purified with filters usually made of wool.

The Romans had three water-supply systems. One system brought water to homes through metered pipes. The meters allowed the head of the water board to send accurate bills to every home for the water used. Another system fed the public baths. A third system supplied the beautiful pools and fountains in the city.

1. Which fact would have led Vitruvius to choose silver for the tanks that held water?
   a. Silver does not affect the quality of water.
   b. Silver is a rare metal.
   c. Making large items from silver is difficult.
   d. Silver is attractive.

2. The Romans probably concluded that wool makes a good filter because it
   a. is dense and thick.
   b. may contain germs from the sheep.
   c. is found everywhere.
   d. never needs to be replaced.

3. From the fact that the Romans had three separate water systems, you can conclude that
   a. they had different degrees of water quality.
   b. they did not build efficiently.
   c. the public baths were not charged for water.
   d. the older systems were no longer usable.

4. Underline a sentence that supports the conclusion that homeowners in ancient Rome probably did not waste water.

Practice Exercise 15

Of all the forces of nature, lightning is perhaps the most feared. The Greeks and Romans believed it was proof that the gods were angry. The Roman god Jupiter, so the story goes, hurled lightning bolts to show his displeasure. In medieval days, witches were thought to cause lightning.

In modern times, many superstitions about lightning have developed. Most of them are about ways to protect yourself from being struck by lightning. Here are some of the most common. No one is killed by lightning when asleep. To be awakened by a streak of lightning is a good sign. If you wind a snake's skin around you, you cannot be struck. It is unlucky to mention lightning right after the flash. A person who looks at lightning may not see well again.

1. Which of the following statements from the selection is probably true?
  a. No one is killed by lightning when asleep.
  b. If you wind a snake's skin around you, you cannot be struck.
  c. It is unlucky to mention lightning right after the flash.
  d. Of all the forces of nature, lightning is one of the most feared.

2. In ancient and medieval times, lightning was seen as
  a. an evil thing.
  b. a bit of good luck.
  c. a reason for celebration.
  d. a sign of change for the better.

3. The conclusions about lightning drawn by the Greeks and Romans were
  a. based on scientific study.
  b. well proven.
  c. reasonable.
  d. based on superstitions.

4. Underline the sentence that best supports the conclusion that there was a time when people were sometimes blamed for lightning.

— Practice Exercise *16* —————————

The army has been interested in homing pigeons for many years. The idea of training pigeons to carry messages to planes in flight was worked out during World War I. In recent years, pigeons have been trained for night flying and for flying over water. It was learned that they would rather fly at night than fly over water. Many pigeons have been trained to carry messages from ships to shore. Some have even been trained to carry messages from shore to ships. Different pigeons fly at different altitudes. Army tests have shown that pigeons fly well even at a height of 35,000 feet (nearly 11,000 meters). At this altitude, pilots need heated suits and oxygen masks.

1. Which fact would have led the army to conclude that pigeons were a good choice for the experiments?
a. Pigeons are easily trained.
b. Pigeons are curious about people.
c. Pigeons are expensive to buy.
d. Pigeons are subject to many diseases.

2. Tests conducted by the army seem to show that pigeons
a. eat very little during long flights.
b. prefer to fly in pairs.
c. fly only during the daytime and only over land.
d. can reach great altitudes.

3. The first two sentences imply that
a. the army has trained many kinds of birds.
b. pigeons fly faster than hawks and ravens.
c. the army is no longer training pigeons.
d. planes in World War I did not have radios.

4. Underline two sentences that suggest that pigeons can survive at very low temperatures.

Practice Exercise 17

Arctic tundra is found in the far north near the Arctic Ocean. It is a flat, treeless area covered by mosses, lichens, grasses, and small shrubs. Tundra often looks like a gray-green plain with many lakes and ponds. In the fall the tundra's colors change to red and brown.

An important part of Arctic tundra is the permafrost layer. This is a layer of frozen water and soil that remains protected all year beneath the top layer of soil and plants. Permafrost prevents water from draining away.

The warm season in the tundra is very short, so the tiny plants can only grow a little bit each year. When people build roads or buildings on tundra, they must be very careful. If the tiny tundra plants are destroyed and the top layer of soil is removed, the permafrost may begin to melt and wash away.

1. You can conclude that you would be likely to find Arctic tundra
   a. wherever rainfall is very heavy.
   b. in cold climates.
   c. in deserts.
   d. in areas below sea level.

2. If you were in a plane flying over an area of tundra in October, the landscape would look most like a
   a. striped banner.
   b. white blanket.
   c. brown velvet rug.
   d. lush, green garden.

3. The plant life of the tundra
   a. acts as a blanket for the soil beneath.
   b. is destroyed every winter.
   c. harms the permafrost layer.
   d. is a tourist attraction.

4. Underline the sentence that supports the correct answer to number 2.

Practice Exercise *18*

Gemstones are identified according to their color, crystal form, luster, and hardness. Color is the first quality noticed in a gemstone. But care should be taken in identifying gems by their colors alone. The colors of some minerals do not change. Many minerals, however, have a wide range of colors. Iron and copper may slightly change the color of some minerals. A better method of identifying gems is through crystal shapes. These shapes form within a certain range of temperatures and pressures. The luster or shine of a mineral may be described as glassy, pearly, greasy, waxy, silky, or brilliant. Hardness is measured by a scratch test. The tester tries to scratch the gemstone with another mineral or with a steel knife blade. The diamond, with a hardness rating of 10, is the hardest mineral known.

1. The writer implies that
   a. the whitest diamonds are always the hardest and most expensive.
   b. a perfect stone is very expensive.
   c. a yellow quartz may be mistaken for a yellow topaz.
   d. most gems have the same crystal shape.

2. From evidence in the passage, you can conclude that
   a. a few minerals are harder than a diamond.
   b. a diamond is a type of quartz.
   c. gems with a high luster are never found in nature.
   d. some gems can be scratched by steel.

3. The passage implies that
   a. 10 is the highest number on the hardness scale.
   b. blue is the most unusual color in gemstones.
   c. jewelers do not test the stones they sell.
   d. rubies are usually a shade of red.

4. Underline a sentence that supports the writer's conclusion that identifying gems by color alone is unwise.

Practice Exercise 19

The dogsled driver may be called a "musher," but the driver never says "mush" to the dogs. In sled-dog language, it's "hike" that means "Let's go!" And that's exactly what hundreds of mushers shouted across the snowy plains of Chub Lake Park in Carlton, Minnesota. It was the Annual Mid-American Sled-Dog Races.

In below-zero weather, seventy-six mushers drove their dogs and sleds for two days on what the pros called a really first-rate track. The trail ran 20 miles (about 32 kilometers) on the flat, snowy surface of the lake; into the rolling, wooded countryside nearby; and finally over the gentle hills of the park from which more than 6,500 people enjoyed a perfect view of the events. The competition was keen and the action was fast, as mushers from all parts of the United States and Canada competed for the honor of bringing in their teams in record time.

1. The driver never says "mush" to the dogs because
   a. they would not understand the word.
   b. they might run too fast.
   c. "mush" is used only in Alaska.
   d. they might turn too quickly.

2. A "first-rate track" probably consists of
   a. heavily drifted snow.
   b. smooth, hard-packed snow.
   c. icy, slippery, crusted snow.
   d. wet, mushy snow.

3. French trappers shouted, *"Marchons!"* to their sled dogs, meaning "Let's go!" This probably led to the conclusion that
   a. dogs are better suited to cold weather than horses.
   b. French dogs are best at pulling sleds.
   c. French drivers make the best competitors in races.
   d. dogsled drivers shouted, "Mush on!" or "Mush!"

4. Underline a sentence that implies that dogsled drivers and spectators are very hardy individuals.

Practice Exercise **20**

Although Santa Claus as we know him is a figure created out of folk customs, the idea for such a generous old fellow can be traced back to a real person. He was a priest named Nicholas and served as the bishop of Myra in Asia Minor in the fourth century. He was a kindly man who inherited a great deal of money and spent it on people in need. Because of his acts of mercy, he became the patron saint of children and sailors. In Greek and Latin churches, the feast of St. Nicholas is celebrated on his birthday, December 6. But the memory of the saint's generosity was never forgotten, and his name was soon connected with the giving of presents. In the Germanic languages, his name became Santa Claus.

Although the bishop of Myra's giving was unexpected, children today plan ahead for Santa's visit. In Holland, children put out a pair of shoes to receive gifts. In the United States, children hang stockings to collect small gifts.

1. The selection supports which one of the following conclusions?
   a. Santa Claus is known in many parts of the world.
   b. Most holidays are based on folk customs.
   c. People who inherit money are kind.
   d. December 6 is the real date of Christmas.

2. You can conclude that the bishop of Myra was
   a. loyal.
   b. brave.
   c. generous.
   d. sincere.

3. If you were in Holland on December 24, you would expect to find children
   a. hanging stockings.
   b. writing letters to Santa Claus.
   c. putting out shoes.
   d. sending money to the bishop of Myra.

4. Underline a sentence that supports the conclusion drawn in number 2.

PART FIVE

Writing Activities

The writing activities that follow will help you understand the characters you read about. The activities will also help you apply that skill to your own writing.

Complete each activity carefully. Your teacher may ask you to work alone or may prefer to have you work with other students. In many cases, you will be asked to write your answers on separate paper. Your teacher may ask you to write those answers in a notebook or journal. Then all your writing activities will be in the same place.

The activities gradually increase in difficulty. Therefore, you should review each completed activity before you begin a new one. Reread the lessons in Parts One and Two (pages 5–17) if you have any questions about drawing conclusions.

Writing Activity 1

Read the following passage from *Black Beauty* by Anna Sewell. A horse that had been treated badly finds a new home.

I was led home, placed in a comfortable stable, fed and left to myself. The next day, when my groom was cleaning my face, he said:

"That is just like the star that Black Beauty had, he is much the same height too; I wonder where he is now."

A little further on he came to the place in my neck where I was bled, and where a little knot was left in the skin. He almost started, and began to look over me carefully, talking to himself.

"White star in the forehead, one white foot on the off side, this little knot just in that place—" then looking at the middle of my back—"and as I am alive, there is that little patch of white hair that John used to call 'Beauty's threepenny bit.' It *must* be Black Beauty! Why, Beauty! Beauty! Do you know me? Little Joe Green." . . . And he began patting and patting me as if he was quite overjoyed.

A. Complete each of the following sentences by drawing a logical conclusion. Remember that a conclusion is a decision or opinion you make that is based on the facts that you read.

1. Black Beauty notes that his stable is comfortable and he was fed.

You can conclude that the stable owners _____

_____

_____.

2. The groom notices that the horse had a star on its face where
Black Beauty had one and is about the same size as Black Beauty.
He then begins to look over the horse more carefully.

You can conclude that the groom _____

_____

_____.

3. Until he thoroughly examines the horse, the groom does not
recognize Black Beauty.

You can conclude that Black Beauty _____

_____

_____.

4. After the groom recognized Black Beauty, he began patting the
horse excitedly.

You can conclude that the groom _____

_____

_____.

5. A comfortable stable, food, and a groom who is an old friend is
what Black Beauty finds at his new home.

You can conclude that Black Beauty _____

_____

_____.

Writing Activity 2

Read the following passage from *Heidi* by Johanna Spyri. A young child's aunt takes her to live with her grandfather.

"She's come to stay with you," Detie told him, coming straight to the point. "I've done all I can for her these four years. Now it's your turn."

"My turn, is it?" snapped the old man, glaring at her. "And when she starts to cry and fret for you, as she's sure to do, what am I supposed to do then?"

"That's your affair," retorted Detie. "Nobody told me how to set about it when she was left on my hands, a baby barely a year old. Goodness knows I had enough to do already, looking after Mother and myself. But now I've got to go away to a job. You're the child's nearest relative. If you can't have her here, do what you like with her. But you'll have to answer for it if she comes to any harm, and I shouldn't think you'd want anything more on your conscience."

Detie was really far from easy in her mind about what she was doing, which was why she spoke so disagreeably, and she had already said more than she meant to.

The old man got up at her last words. She was quite frightened by the way he looked at her, and took a few steps backward.

A. On a separate piece of paper or in your writing notebook, answer the following questions. Your teacher may want you to share your answers with the class. Remember to refer back to the details in the passage when answering the questions.

1. Heidi has lived with Detie for four years. Detie says that Heidi's closest relative is her grandfather. What conclusions can you draw about Heidi's parents?

2. Grandfather wants to know what he will do when Heidi cries for Detie. Does her grandfather have much experience caring for children? Is Heidi likely to miss Detie? Why or why not?

3. Think about the conversation between Detie and her uncle. Have Detie and her uncle seen each other recently? Do they seem to like one another? Why do they speak to each other so rudely?

4. Detie is leaving Heidi with her grandfather after taking care of her for four years. Do you think Detie enjoyed taking care of Heidi? Do you think she cares about what happens to Heidi? Is it likely that Detie loves Heidi?

B. Think about the kind of care a five-year-old child needs. On a separate piece of paper or in your writing notebook, list all the needs a child has and how these can be met. Using the list, write a set of instructions that Detie might give to Heidi's grandfather to help him care for Heidi.

Writing Activity 3

Read the following passage. In it a young man remembers a summer of drought.

Although I was old enough to help out on the ranch, my summer days were still filled with freedom. My friends and I spent hours playing at Old Mile Long Creek. It was our Mississippi River, where we rode steamboats down to New Orleans. It was the Amazon, where we explored the shores in search of new animal species. Most of our new species were frogs that we examined and then put into the water. It was our Atlantic Ocean, where we rescued passengers from a sinking ship. Again, frogs were "the passengers" we rescued. It was our rock-skipping place. It was the place where we cooled our feet on a hot summer afternoon.

This summer was different, though. Every day, the sun beat down on the land. The creek was mostly just a trickle of water in a dry bed. There were no frogs to be seen. They seemed to have disappeared. This had to be the hottest summer ever, and the driest one, too.

Then the storm hit. Everywhere you looked the ranch was hopping! I mean it was really hopping. Frogs were everywhere. They seemed to be jumping for glee. Water ran off the hard dry land into the creek bed. Once again the creek rippled with water. Once again the night was filled with the songs of croaking frogs. The ground softened and thirstily soaked up the water. The grass turned green. The drought ended. My friends and I returned to the Mississippi, the Amazon, and the Atlantic Ocean.

A. Answer each of the following questions by drawing a logical conclusion. Remember that a conclusion is a decision or opinion you make that is based on the facts that you read.

1. Does the boy live in an urban or rural area? What clues does the story give?

2. The boy calls the creek the Mississippi River, the Amazon River, and the Atlantic Ocean. What did the creek represent to the boy and his friends?

3. Frogs live on land and in the water. Why might they be hard to find during a drought?

4. The boy said that after the rain fell, frogs were everywhere. Why might the frogs be everywhere after the storm ended the drought?

5. Do you think the boy and his friends really returned to the Mississippi River, the Amazon, and the Atlantic Ocean? Explain your answer.

B. The passage describes a summer that a young man remembers. Think about last summer. On a separate sheet of paper, write something that you remember about the summer. Maybe you went on a vacation with your family. Maybe the summer was hotter or cooler than usual. Maybe it was just another summer. Tell something about your summer.

Writing Activity 4

Read the following passage from *Round the Moon* by Jules Verne. Published in 1870, this science-fiction story tells about space explorers who circle the moon and return to Earth. Searchers had lost hope of finding the space capsule and the travelers inside it after days of searching for it under water.

All had forgotten this fundamental law, namely, that on account of its specific lightness, the projectile, after having been drawn by its fall to the greatest depth of the ocean, must naturally return to the surface. And now it was floating quietly at the mercy of the waves.

The boats were put to sea. . . . Excitement was at its height! Every heart beat loudly while they advanced to the projectile. What did it contain? Living or dead?

Living, yes! Living, at least unless death had struck Barbicane and his two friends since they hoisted the flag. . . .

A boat came alongside. It was J. T. Matson's, and he rushed to the broken window.

At that moment they heard a clear and merry voice; the voice of Michel Arden, exclaiming in an accent of triumph:

"White all, Barbicane, white all!"

Barbicane, Michel Arden, and Nicholl were playing at dominoes!

A. On a separate piece of paper or in your writing notebook, answer the following questions. Refer back to the passage to check your answers. If you are unfamiliar with any of the words in the passage, look them up in a dictionary or discuss them with your teacher before you begin writing.

1. Why did the capsule float? Why did the searchers expect to find the capsule under water?

2. Searchers feared that the space travelers might no longer be alive. Why do you think they thought the travelers had not survived? What do you think Matson was feeling as he approached the capsule?

3. Do you think the space travelers were concerned about their safety? Explain your answer. How do you think they reacted when they saw Matson peeking into their capsule?

B. Jules Verne wrote *Round the Moon,* a sequel to his *From the Earth to the Moon,* about 100 years before astronauts actually circled and landed on the moon. Imagine that you are a reporter who is writing about the space travelers and their return to Earth. List questions you might ask the space travelers and the rescuers. Use the questions to help you write a short news article about the event.

Writing Activity 5

Read the following passage from *The Strange Case of Dr. Jekyll and Mr. Hyde* by Robert Louis Stevenson. In the classic story, a good doctor becomes "Mr. Hyde," his ugly, evil alter ego. In the passage, Jekyll's lawyer visits his home to discuss why he would leave his fortune to such an unpleasant young man.

Mr. Utterson, Jekyll's lawyer, was ashamed of his relief, when Poole presently returned to announce that Dr. Jekyll was gone out.

"I saw Mr. Hyde go in by the old dissecting-room door, Poole," he said. "Is that right, when Dr. Jekyll is from home?"

"Quite right, Mr. Utterson, sir," replied the servant. "Mr. Hyde has a key."

"Your master seems to have a great deal of trust in that young man, Poole," resumed the other musingly.

"Yes, sir, he do indeed," said Poole. "We have all orders to obey him."

"I do not think I ever met Mr. Hyde?" asked Utterson.

"O, dear no, sir. He never *dines* here," replied the butler. "Indeed we see very little of him on this side of the house; he mostly comes and goes by the laboratory." . . .

And the lawyer set out homeward with a very heavy heart. "Poor Henry Jekyll," he thought, "my mind misgives me he is in deep waters!"

A. Answer each of the following questions by drawing a logical conclusion.

1. Why would the lawyer be somewhat relieved that Dr. Jekyll was not at home?

2. Why would Dr. Jekyll give a key to his home to Mr. Hyde?

3. Why might the doctor's servants have been told to obey Mr. Hyde? How do you think they reacted to this order?

4. Dr. Jekyll often had old friends to dinner. Why might Hyde never join the group?

5. Why might the lawyer think that Dr. Jekyll is in trouble?

B. Dr. Jekyll and Mr. Hyde were two sides of the same person—one good, one bad. Some people think that everyone and everything has some good and some bad in them. Write a paragraph or two telling whether you agree that there is good or bad in everything or everyone. Give reasons for your opinion.

Writing Activity 6

A. Sue Tan started to shake as she hurried down the crowded sidewalk toward city hall. Her meeting with the mayor was in five minutes.

On a separate piece of paper or in your writing notebook, describe what happens to Sue Tan. Why is she meeting the mayor? Why is she shaking? What can you conclude about Sue Tan? Is she wearing a hidden microphone? Your paragraph should lead a reader to a reasonable conclusion.

B. Ask another student to read your paragraph and have him or her draw a conclusion. Do you agree with the conclusion? Is the conclusion logical? What in your writing helped the student draw that conclusion?

ANSWER KEY

Practice Exercise 1

1. d   2. c   3. c

4. He was known by that name to the nation. Also known to the nation were Tad's pranks.

Practice Exercise 2

1. a   2. b   3. d

4. The koala is a gentle little animal.

Practice Exercise 3

1. d   2. d   3. b

4. Each dugout would keep a family safe through the winter until the Pilgrims could build log cabins in the spring.

Practice Exercise 4

1. a   2. b   3. d

4. In most cases, however, they stop quickly with no side effects.

Practice Exercise 5

1. c   2. d   3. c

4. Most people do not think of a toad as a desert dweller because they know that toads must be born in water.

Practice Exercise 6

1. a   2. b   3. a

4. Plankton is made up of the tiniest plants and animals in the sea.

Practice Exercise 7

1. a   2. d   3. c
4. Sometimes there is coral with razor-sharp edges.

Practice Exercise 8

1. a   2. d   3. a
4. When wolves come close, the oxen defend themselves by forming a ring with their sharp horns pointed outward.

Practice Exercise 9

1. b   2. d   3. b
4. They think of their dogs as their transportation and their friends.

Practice Exercise 10

1. c   2. d   3. b
4. One person might have been tall and had long feet. Another person might have been short and had short feet.

Practice Exercise 11

1. a   2. d   3. c
4. But a lot more sugar is needed to make ice cream and other cold foods taste sweet.

Practice Exercise 12

1. c   2. d   3. b
4. The shipbuilders were sure that the *Titanic* could not sink because of its special design.

Practice Exercise 13

1. a   2. d   3. c
4. John's brother, Edwin Thomas Booth, is remembered as one of the greatest actors in the history of American theater. John Wilkes Booth was also a promising actor.

Practice Exercise 14

1. a   2. a   3. a

4. The meters allowed the head of the water board to send accurate bills to every home for the water used.

Practice Exercise 15

1. d   2. a   3. d

4. In medieval days, witches were thought to cause lightning.

Practice Exercise 16

1. a   2. d   3. d

4. Army tests have shown that pigeons fly well even at a height of 35,000 feet (nearly 11,000 meters). At this altitude, pilots need heated suits and oxygen masks.

Practice Exercise 17

1. b   2. c   3. a

4. In the fall the tundra's colors change to red and brown.

Practice Exercise 18

1. c   2. d   3. a

4. Many minerals, however, have a wide range of colors; *or,* Iron and copper may slightly change the color of some minerals.

Practice Exercise 19

1. a   2. b   3. d

4. In below-zero weather, seventy-six mushers drove their dogs and sleds for two days on what the pros called a really first-rate track.

Practice Exercise 20

1. a   2. c   3. c

4. He was a kindly man who inherited a great deal of money and spent it on people in need; *or,* Because of his acts of mercy, he became the patron saint of children and sailors.

PROGRESS CHART

Practice Exercise Number	Put an X through the number of each question answered correctly.				Total Number Correct
	Question	Question	Question	Question	
1	1	2	3	4	
2	1	2	3	4	
3	1	2	3	4	
4	1	2	3	4	
5	1	2	3	4	
6	1	2	3	4	
7	1	2	3	4	
8	1	2	3	4	
9	1	2	3	4	
10	1	2	3	4	
11	1	2	3	4	
12	1	2	3	4	
13	1	2	3	4	
14	1	2	3	4	
15	1	2	3	4	
16	1	2	3	4	
17	1	2	3	4	
18	1	2	3	4	
19	1	2	3	4	
20	1	2	3	4	

Total of correct answers for all 20 exercises:

Rating: 70–80 Excellent
55–69 Good
40–54 Fair